THE HIDDEN
MASCOTS™

FIND BIG AL!®

Art Direction and Creation by
Kristen Wood and Kim Wewers
Illustrated by Anna Terry

Published by My Campus Adventure, Incorporated

www.mycampusadventure.com

Find the Hidden Mascots is a trademark of
My Campus Adventure, Incorporated.

ISBN 978-1-935159-10-0

BIG AL

CRIMSON TIDE AND BIG AL

The official mascot for the University of Alabama is the Crimson Tide. The first nickname for the University of Alabama was the "Thin Red Line" which came from the crimson colored uniforms. This nickname was used until 1906 when a sports writer for the Birmingham Age-Herald referred to the Alabama team as the "Crimson Tide" after a hard fought game against Auburn University.

The Alabama-Auburn game was the last game of the season. It was played in a sea of mud and Auburn was favored to win. Alabama played a great game in the red mud and held Auburn to a 6-6 tie. Since that game, they have been known as the Crimson Tide.

The Crimson Tide became associated with the "elephant" in 1930 when the Alabama team, coached by Coach Wade, was considered a powerful, big tough, fast and aggressive team. During the Ole Miss game that year, the Alabama team was returning to the field and it is said that the earth started to tremble and there was a distant rumble. A fan from the stands was heard to yell, "Hold your horses, the elephants are coming," and out stampeded the Alabama varsity!

Today, the Crimson Tide has a costumed mascot elephant named Big Al. Big Al made his first debut at the 1979 Sugar Bowl. He attends all home games and helps get the Bama fans fired up for the games!!

Did You Know?

The Bryant-Denny Stadium has been the home stadium to Alabama football since 1929. Holding 92,138 fans, it is the fifth largest stadium in the Southeastern conference. Alabama has had consecutive sell out home games since 1988.

ROLL TIDE!

Did You Know?

The Crimson Tide football team first gained recognition in 1922 when Coach Wallace Wade became head coach. In 1925, Coach Wade led the team to its first undefeated season and its first Rose Bowl invitation, which they won in an upset against Washington, 20 -19.

Did You Know?

Tailgating is an important part of gameday tradition. "Kick-off on the Quad" begins three hours before kick-off and takes place on the Quad at the Alabama campus. There are fun activities, food and games. The cheerleaders and dance teams perform to get the crowd pumped up for the game!

The Alabama batter hits a line drive as the runner from 3rd base scores the winning run! Can you find Big Al and these items?

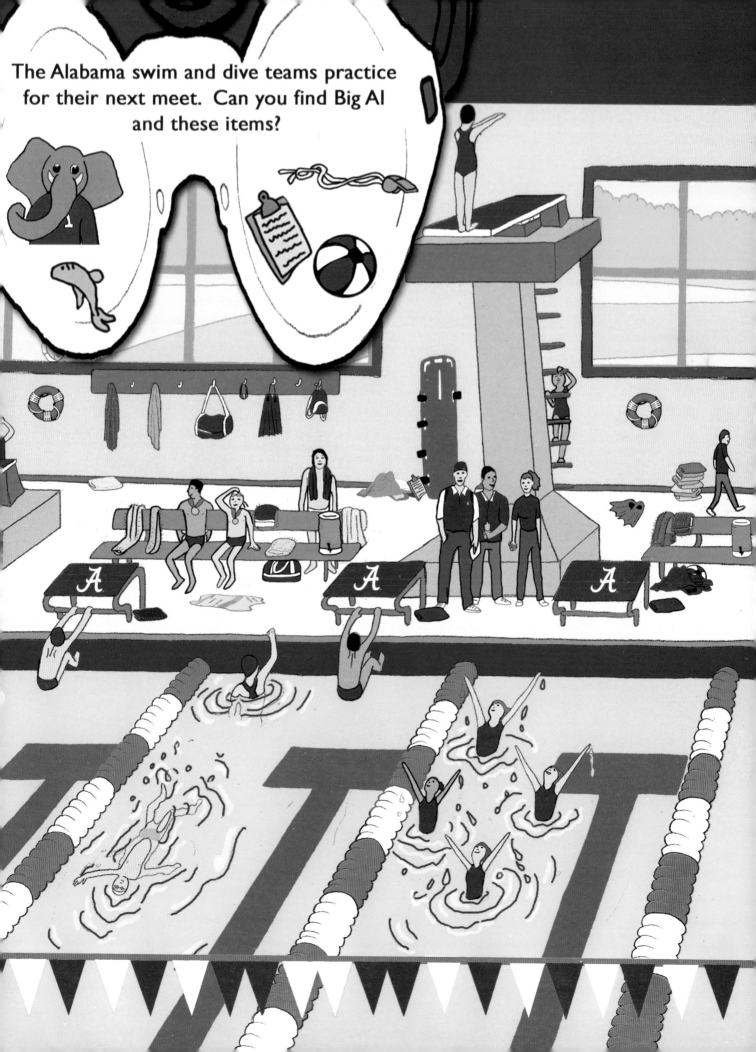

The Alabama swim and dive teams practice for their next meet. Can you find Big Al and these items?

Can you find Big Al and these items in the scene?

The locker room is where the players get fired up
to play for the win! Can you find Big Al
and these items in the locker room?

The Alabama volleyball team warms up with spikes and volleys before their big game. Can you find Big Al and these items?

GORGAS LIBRARY

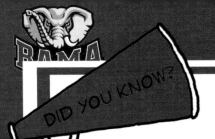

The University of Alabama "Million Dollar Band" is an exciting part of Crimson Tide spirit and tradition. The Band is known for its colorful halftime shows and has appeared on television more often than any other college band.

Don't miss kick-off! Return to the football game and find these items:

#1 Finger
Player #20
Microphone
Saxophone
Camera
4 Footballs

Get ready for the game. Head to the locker room to find these items:

Whistle
Wrist Bands
Tooth Brush
Bar of Soap
Soccer Ball
Mouthguard

The distinctive script "A" logo represents the vast tradition of the University of Alabama.

Can you go back and find 5 Alabama logos in each scene?

Grab your putter and return to the green! Can you find these items?

Deer
Squirrel
2 Blue Birds
Ice
Quiet Sign

Dribble back to the
court and look for
these items:

10 Basketballs
Player # 14
#1 Finger
3 Tubas
Whistle
Pair of Green Shoes

DID YOU KNOW?

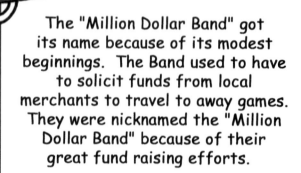

The "Million Dollar Band" got
its name because of its modest
beginnings. The Band used to have
to solicit funds from local
merchants to travel to away games.
They were nicknamed the "Million
Dollar Band" because of their
great fund raising efforts.

Skip back to the library
and check out these
items:

Mouse
Water Bottle
Pencil
Yellow Pad of Paper
Clock

Dive back into the swimming
pool and locate these
items:

Megaphone
Goggles
Blue Flippers
4 Gold Medals
Pom Pom
Camera

DID YOU KNOW?

A great Alabama tradition is the
"Walk of Champions." Every home
game, approximately 2.5 hours before
kickoff, the team buses pull up to the
North end of Bryant-Denny Stadium.
Fans gather and cheer for the Crimson
Tide team as they exit the bus and
walk into the locker rooms to get them
fired up for the game!

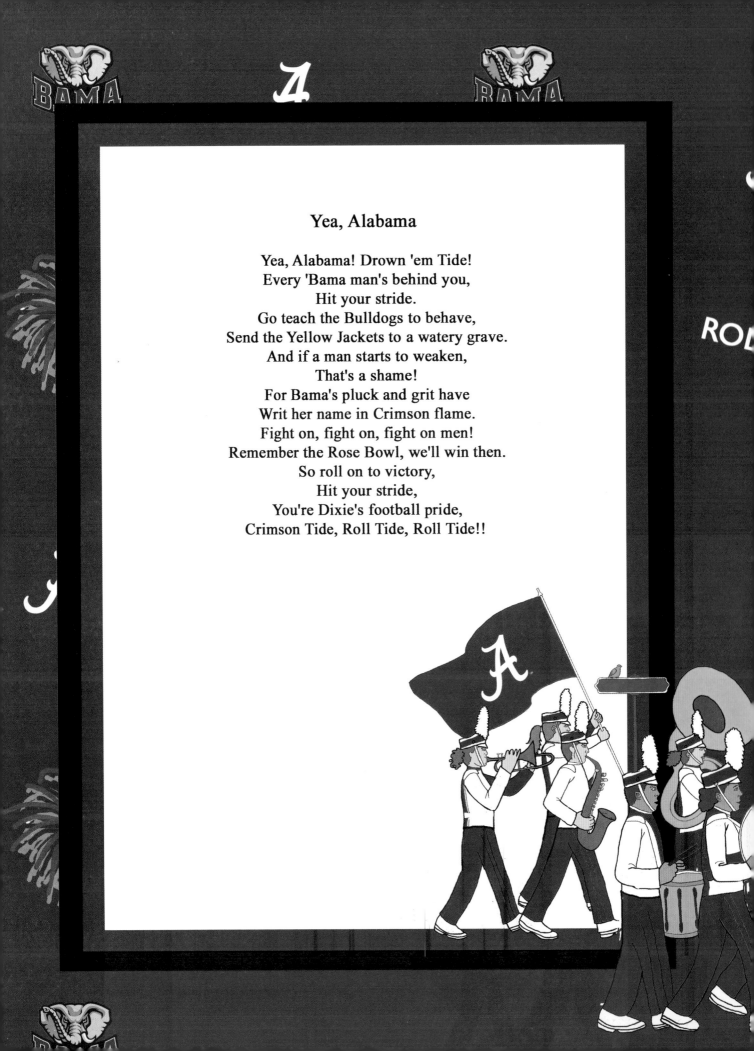

Yea, Alabama

Yea, Alabama! Drown 'em Tide!
Every 'Bama man's behind you,
Hit your stride.
Go teach the Bulldogs to behave,
Send the Yellow Jackets to a watery grave.
And if a man starts to weaken,
That's a shame!
For Bama's pluck and grit have
Writ her name in Crimson flame.
Fight on, fight on, fight on men!
Remember the Rose Bowl, we'll win then.
So roll on to victory,
Hit your stride,
You're Dixie's football pride,
Crimson Tide, Roll Tide, Roll Tide!!